THE COACH AS A LEADER

ISBN 979-8-88751-950-0 (paperback)
ISBN 979-8-88751-951-7 (digital)

Christian Faith Publishing
832 Park Avenue
Meadville, PA 16335
www.christianfaithpublishing.com

Illustrated by Earljohn Desuasido

Printed in the United States of America

THE COACH AS A LEADER

Cristina Bejar

"Hello, David." Mary indicated the chair in front of him. "I have called you here because I wanted to talk about your progress in the organization."

David settled himself in the chair. "Thanks, Mary."

"How are you?"

"I'm great! Busy as usual, but our latest project with marketing really went well, so I am happy."

Mary smiled. "I saw your team's work, and I thought it was amazing. You have done a good job, and I am proud of you."

David beamed. "Thanks!"

"You're welcome! Now, as I have said, I wanted to talk about your progress in the organization."

"I'm all ears!"

"Great!" Mary nodded. "Have you ever thought about where the word *coach* came from?"

David raised his eyebrows and looked at his leader. "Sports?"

Mary smiled. "Some would think so too, but no." She chuckled. "You know, a long time ago, *coaches* were conveyances that carried people or goods from one place to another. It used to be pulled by horses and driven by a driver that eventually got called the *coach* for the vehicle he was driving."

"I didn't know that." David scratched his head.

"That's okay! This is more common knowledge in other parts of the world like Great Britain." She smiled. "Anyway, the coach usually has a destination to reach. This is determined before the actual journey is undertaken." Mary paused. "What do you think the destination stands for?"

David took a minute to think about it. "A goal?"

Mary beamed. "That's right!"

"A coach has a *team* of horses that pulls the carriage."

David looked surprised. "Is that where the word *team* comes from?"

"Well, I am not sure, but I do know that a set of horses pulling a carriage is called a team." Mary smiled again.

"Wow. I never thought of that."

"You see, the coach knows each horse on his team, and he knows how to arrange them accordingly so that they could function to the best of their abilities." Mary leaned forward. "Horses, like humans, have their own quirks, temperaments, strengths, and weaknesses."

"Go on." David sat up straighter in his chair.

"The horse can be likened to a technical expert or a specialist." Mary looked at David intently. "What do you think the horse's specialization or expertise is?"

"Hmmm, to run?"

"Bravo!" Mary exclaimed. "What is your expertise, David?"

"I'm a graphic artist."

"That's right!"

David furrowed his brows. "I don't think I like being compared to a horse."

Mary bent her head to the side, "Why?"

"Well, because I am human, and humans can think and interact."

Mary nodded. "You are right, of course." Mary thought for a moment. "When you think about it, the objective cannot be met at the most efficient time without the horse's capability to run fast. Can you imagine if the driver or the coach has to pull the carriage all by himself?"

David thought for a moment. "It would be hard, the coach does not have the strength nor the speed."

"Uh-huh. The horses are very important to the success of the mission, like you are very important to this organization as a technical expert in your field. The beauty of it is that because you are not only an expert like a horse is, but being human, you are developable for other functions." Mary smiled. "But more on that later."

"Okay." David nodded.

"Horses usually have very simple needs—food, water, and the need to procreate. What do you think you or other employees need in the organization?"

"I guess if you put it that way, we need compensation, benefits, rewards, etc."

"You are right, again!" Mary snapped her fingers. "The coach understands the needs of the horses and so to keep them focused on the objective of getting to the destination, the coach has to put blinders on them so they do not get distracted while they run. They are also harnessed so they run together as a team. What do you think the blinders and harnesses stand for?"

David shook his head. "I don't know."

"That's okay. Usually it's policies, procedures, guidelines—in an organization, these are very important to keep the employees focused on their jobs so they could meet the objectives."

"Ah! Right!" David nodded. He frowned. "I still could not get over being likened to a horse."

Mary smiled sympathetically. "I understand it might make you feel uncomfortable, being compared to a horse, but like I said earlier, what sets you apart from a horse is your developability."

"Developability?"

"Yes. You see, most organizations are so appreciative of their individual contributors or technical specialists that they promote them to supervisory positions without the proper preparation."

"Huh?"

"Can you imagine promoting a horse to the position of driver?"

"That's so weird!"

"Well, because a horse is a horse, it is impossible! But you, being human, can be promoted to supervisor from being a technical expert."

"Oh!"

"However, if we bring it back to the analogy of the horse, the horse has to go through a thorough transformation to become a coach." Mary leaned on her table. "I believe that every person, before he/she gets promoted, must first go through development to train them to become leaders," she finished quietly.

"I get it now." David clasped his hands together.

"You see, if you start thinking of yourself as a coach rather than a technical expert, your perspective would change."

David nodded. "It's a little difficult right now, given that I am only that."

"True, but the reason why we are talking right now is that I would like to prepare you to lead your own team."

David clutched his heart suddenly. "Really?"

"Yes, really."

"Wow! I mean, when?" David grinned from ear to ear.

"When your transformation is complete."

David laughed out loud. "When I am no longer a horse?" He laughed again.

Mary nodded. "It is very important that you understand the responsibilities of a coach before you can become a leader."

"Thank you."

"You're welcome."

"So apart from making sure that I am adept at the policies, procedures, and guidelines, what else should I know?"

Mary gave a thumbs up. "Spot on!"

They both laughed.

"The coach is responsible for the physical arrangement of the horses. He knows which horse should go front, left, and back because he is mindful of the dynamics of the horses with each other. He knows that arranging them accordingly would make them run long distances more efficiently."

"Even that is a consideration for a leader?" David asked wonderingly.

"Of course! Not only that, the coach must sit behind the horses in an elevated chair at all times. Why do you think so?"

"So that he can see the horizon and watch the horses at the same time?"

"You are absolutely right!" Mary chuckled. "The coach as the driver must have a clear view of the road. This can be likened to a *vision*. He maintains this vision at all times and *directs* his horses unwaveringly. This is the reason why a coach or a leader is called a *supervisor—super*, meaning higher or greater, and *visor* meaning *vision*."

"I'm learning so much!" David shook his head. "So that's what a supervisor means."

Mary laughed delightedly. "Yes!" Mary leaned back on her chair again. "What do you think the coach has to do if he wants his horses to run faster?"

"Uh, use a whip?"

"Right again! Now, some people think that the whip is used to hit the horses. That could not be farther from the truth. How do you think the whip is used?"

"I don't know. I thought it was to hit them, but you said it's not."

"Think of it. If the coach were to hit the horses, they would get injured because the whip is made of very stiff leather. Perhaps there are coaches that truly hit their horses, and it is true that the horses run faster because of the pain. Do you think the horses and the coach would reach their destination quicker if the coach hits them?"

"Yes," David answered uncertainly.

"Yes, they would. That is why autocratic leaderships where leaders hurt, threaten, or bully the employees so that they could do more or achieve more is effective. However, it is effective only for the short term because eventually, workers get stressed, mentally and physically, and will not be able to function productively in the long term with the same efficiency or effectiveness. So, for the sake of sustainability, a coach must never hit the horses."

"Then what is the whip for?" David asked.

KRACK!!!

"The coach uses the whip only for the cracking sound it makes above the horses' heads. This is sufficient for the horses to run faster." Mary smiled. "What do you think the coach does with the reins?"

"Pull them?" David made a pulling gesture.

"You want the horses to go faster, but you pull the reins?"

"Oh, no! He has to loosen the reins!"

"Right! Why?"

"So, they have freedom to move!"

"Exactly! The coach has to slacken the reins—without letting go (he still has to maintain control) so that the horses would have enough freedom to run. Likewise, in the corporate setting, leaders who want their employees to work harder and produce better must give consistent feedback and enough freedom for the latter to *fly* or *soar* to greater heights of productivity."

"Amazing!"

"Indeed!" Mary was silent after that, then she asked, "What happens if one of the horses on the team gets injured? Will the coach, who once was a horse, vacate his seat and function once again as a horse?"

David shook his head. "No."

"Why not?"

"Who will drive the team if he does?"

"Absolutely! At all costs, the coach must never leave his position of supervision. If he has to take out the horse that is injured then he has to rearrange the team to *run* without that horse. An injured horse can slow down the team and must be given the right attention—whether to be brought to the horse hospital, or in the olden times, the horse is shot if he becomes lame because it *is more costly to keep a nonperforming horse. This is especially true considering* the amount of food and care that he would require as compared to his ability to contribute to the objective of pulling the conveyance to the destination."

"How brutal!"

"Well, I actually asked a horse breeder about this, and she said that it is actually showing mercy to the horse to put it down because the pain it has to endure while lame is excruciating. Just think about the weight of a horse's body and the size of his legs. What do you think about the hard calls that a supervisor must make about non-performing employees?"

"I think nonperforming employees must be given enough time to improve."

"That is a good answer." Mary nodded encouragingly. "I want you to think about the team. What is the impact of a nonperforming employee or an employee that is behaviorally challenged to the team?"

"Like you said a while ago, it will slow the team down."

"Correct. So your role as a supervisor is to identify nonperforming employees or behaviorally challenged employees and make a decision whether you will invest time to help them improve, isolate them from the team, or transfer them to where they can contribute better, or even separate them from the organization. Making the hard calls is the decision that the coach must make."

"So much responsibility!" David exclaimed.

"That is true. Becoming a leader is not an easy thing. How do you feel so far?"

"I'm excited and daunted at the same time."

"I could imagine. When I first became a supervisor myself, I was very unprepared. I made so many mistakes along the way. I do not want you to go through that yourself."

"Thanks, Mary. I really appreciate the talk so far."

"We're not done yet," she laughed.

"Please continue."

"The team cannot be expected to run the entire time with a missing horse. The coach still has to make sure that the injured one is taken care of and a replacement found the soonest possible time. Why is this so?"

"Because it is a burden to the other members of the team to make up for the absence?"

"Right! Even if the team could function without the missing horse and still reach the destination, they would be stretched and would not become as efficient nor as effective as when the team was complete if they are expected to do this again and again. For the sake of sustainability, each horse should only be expected to run at his/her optimum capability and not more. Likewise, in an organization, each employee must attend to his/her key result area and performance indicators without doing more because of the absence of a colleague. You, with the help of human resources, must be able to fill in the vacancy the soonest time possible. Never should you say, "Hey! They can do it, why hire another?" If sustainability is important to the business, then finding a qualified replacement is imperative. What do you think?"

"I'll remember this, for sure."

"Good!" Mary nodded her approval. "Say for example, there was no injury, and the coach and team arrive at the destination, what should the coach do next?"

"Give the horses food and water?"

"Yes! They must be watered and fed, brushed down, blanketed, and given sufficient rest, probably given an apple or a carrot. Why?"

"Because the next day, they are expected to run again."

"Perfect! In an organization, the promised compensation and benefits have to be given to ensure that the employees are still engaged to continue working and producing as they are expected. It is important to note that at down times or rest times, the coach must spend time with each horse to give it feedback or tender care. Likewise, you must spend time with each employee to meet their personal needs of being treated with respect, appreciated, and valued. If necessary, you must be able to listen and respond with empathy if the employee has a concern. It would be ideal if you could involve each member of the team in the means and ways of how to achieve the objective."

Mary paused. "David, what do you think?"

"I think it is scary and exciting at the same time, but I am no longer thinking of myself as a horse. I would like to lead and be able to apply what I have learned today. Thanks, Mary!"

"You're welcome. Starting today, I would like you to think about your individual development plan. Check in with me next month, and we will discuss what support you need. I would be happy to guide you in your development as a supervisor."

What are your career aspirations for the next three years?

Example: Become a certified executive coach and consultant for one of the top five-hundred companies in the next three years.

____

____

____

____

What are the eligibility requirements of that role?

Example: Certified executive coach, post-graduate degree, fifteen years work experience in a corporate setting

____

____

____

____

____

____

____

____

____

____

____

____

____

____

What are the traits or competencies you need to be suitable for that role?

Example: Takes initiative—the tendency to perceive what is necessary to be accomplished and to proceed on one's own

____

____

____

____

____

____

____

____

____

____

____

____

____

____

What are your action plans to get there?

Goal: ____

Example: Become a certified executive coach and be a consultant for one of the top five-hundred companies in the next three years.

Activity	Measurement	Due Date	Resources
Example: 1. Attend all training sessions on coaching 2. Participate in company-initiated coaching circles 3. Attend a certification course on executive coaching	Example: Certificate	Example: Certification accomplished within the next three years	LinkedIn courses International certification recognized worldwide training and development team coaching circle

What are your career aspirations for the next five years?

____

____

____

____

What are the eligibility requirements of that role?

____

____

____

____

____

____

____

____

____

____

____

____

What are the traits or competencies you need to be suitable for that role?

____

____

____

____

____

____

____

____

____

____

____

____

____

____

What are your action plans to get there?

Goal			
Activity	Measurement	Due Date	Resources

What are your career aspirations for the next ten years?

____

____

____

____

____

____

____

____

____

____

____

What are the eligibility requirements of that role?

____

____

____

____

____

____

____

____

____

____

____

What are the traits and competencies you need to be suitable for that role?

What are your action plans to get there?

Goal			
Activity	Measurement	Due Date	Resources

About the Author

Cristina, as she prefers to be called, is an experienced professional—skilled in training and development for a Fortune 200 company. Her passion for the people side of things has afforded her the opportunity to serve as an innovative learning and development leader, delivering a wide range of employee-focused, performance-based solutions aligned with organizational objectives. She has a demonstrated history of leading teams through complex project delivery methodologies with strong creative problem-solving skills including performance management, design/implementation, and leadership across a variety of learning and development areas from strategic planning to business implementation.